THE ✦ HOUND

OF ✦ HEAVEN

Francis Thompson

THE • HOUND
OF • HEAVEN

Illustrated by Tim Ladwig

McCracken Press
New York

McCracken Press™
An imprint of Multi Media Communicators, Inc.
575 Madison Avenue, Suite 1006
New York, NY 10022

Printed in the United States of America

ISBN 1-56977-525-7

10 9 8 7 6 5 4 3 2 1

First Edition

This wildly romantic nineteenth-century poem,

first published in England in 1890, portrays

the poet's soul, ravaged by alcohol and drugs,

running away from God who relentlessly

pursues him like a hound on the hunt.

Francis Thompson

Francis Thompson

FRANCIS THOMPSON (1859-1907), a poet of modest reputation who lived in Victorian England, was a victim of his own weak nature. His father wanted him to study medicine; but the young man refused. He went to London to find fame and fortune in the world of literature. There he found he couldn't support himself by his verse. Eventually he fell prey to opium, paying for the powdery packets by selling matches. A religious man, he never lost his faith in God, even while in the grips of the hallucinatory drug. Rescued by a friend who also promised to publish his poems, Thompson survived, managing to write the poem of his life, "The Hound of Heaven," in which he described God's relentless pursuit of his tattered, drug-infected soul, using the metaphor of God as a bounding mastiff.

THE ◆ HOUND
OF ◆ HEAVEN

I fled Him, down the nights and down the days;

I fled Him, down the arches of the years;

I fled Him, down the labyrinthine ways

  Of my own mind; and in the mist of tears

I hid from Him, and under running laughter.

      Up vistaed hopes I sped;

      And shot, precipitated,

Adown Titanic glooms of chasmèd fears,

  From those strong Feet that followed,
        followed after.

      But with unhurrying chase,

      And unperturbèd pace,

    Deliberate speed, majestic instancy,

      They beat — and a Voice beat

      More instant than the Feet —

'All things betray thee, who betrayest Me.'

I pleaded, outlaw-wise,

By many a hearted casement, curtained red,

Trellised with intertwining charities;

(For, though I knew His love Who followèd,

Yet I was sore adread

Lest, having Him, I must have naught beside.)

But, if one little casement parted wide,

The gust of His approach would clash it to:

Fear wist not to evade, as Love wist to pursue.

Across the margent of the world I fled,

And troubled the gold gateways of the stars,

Smiting for shelter on their clangèd bars;

Fretted to dulcet jars

And silvern chatter the pale ports o' the moon.

I said to Dawn: Be sudden — to Eve: Be soon;

With thy young skiey blossoms heap me over

From this tremendous Lover —

Float thy vague veil about me, lest He see!
  I tempted all His servitors, but to find
My own betrayal in their constancy,
In faith to Him their fickleness to me,
  Their traitorous trueness, and their loyal deceit.
To all swift things for swiftness did I sue;
  Clung to the whistling mane of every wind.
    But whether they swept, smoothly fleet,
    The long savannahs of the blue;
      Or whether, Thunder-driven,
    They clanged his chariot 'thwart a heaven,
Plashy with flying lightnings round the spurn o'
    their feet: —
  Fear wist not to evade as Love wist to pursue.
    Still with unhurrying chase,
    And unperturbèd pace,
  Deliberate speed, majestic instancy,
    Came on the following Feet,
    And a Voice above their beat —
  'Naught shelters thee, who wilt not shelter
    Me.'

I sought no more that after which I strayed
    In face of man or maid;
But still within the little children's eyes
    Seems something, something that replies,
They at least are for me, surely for me!
I turned me to them very wistfully;
But just as their young eyes grew sudden fair
    With dawning answers there,
Their angel plucked them from me by the hair.
'Come then, ye other children, Nature's — share
With me' (said I) 'your delicate fellowship;
    Let me greet you lip to lip,
    Let me twine with you caresses,
      Wantoning
    With our Lady-Mother's vagrant tresses,
      Banqueting
    With her in her wind-walled palace,
    Underneath her azured daïs,
    Quaffing, as your taintless way is,
      From a chalice
Lucent-weeping out of the dayspring.'

So it was done:

I in their delicate fellowship was one —

Drew the bolt of Nature's secrecies.

    I knew all the swift importings

    On the wilful space of skies;

    I knew how the clouds arise

    Spumèd of the wild sea-snortings;

      All that's born or dies

    Rose and drooped with; made them shapers

Of mine own moods, or wailful or divine;

    With them joyed and was bereaven.

    I was heavy with the even,

    When she lit her glimmering tapers

    Round the day's dead sanctities.

    I laughed in the morning's eyes.

I triumphed and I saddened with all weather,
    Heaven and I wept together,
And its sweet tears were salt with mortal mine;
Against the red throb of its sunset-heart
    I laid my own to beat,
    And share commingling heat;
But not by that, by that, was eased my human
      smart.
In vain my tears were wet on Heaven's grey cheek.
For ah! we know not what each other says,
    These things and I; in sound *I* speak —
Their sound is but their stir, they speak by silences.
Nature, poor stepdame, cannot slake my drouth;
    Let her, if she would owe me,
Drop yon blue bosom-veil of sky, and show me
    The breasts o' her tenderness:
Never did any milk of hers once bless
      My thirsting mouth.
      Nigh and nigh draws the chase,
      With unperturbèd pace,
    Deliberate speed, majestic instancy;
      And past those noisèd Feet
      A voice comes yet more fleet —
    'Lo! naught contents thee, who content'st
      not Me.'

Naked I wait Thy love's uplifted stroke!
My harness piece by piece Thou hast hewn
　　　from me,
　　　And smitten me to thy knee;
　　I am defenceless utterly.
　　I slept, methinks, and woke,
And, slowly gazing, find me stripped in sleep.
In the rash lustihead of my young powers,
　　I shook the pillaring hours
And pulled my life upon me; grimed with smears,
I stand amid the dust o' the mounded years—
My mangled youth lies dead beneath the heap.
My days have crackled and gone up in smoke,
Have puffed and burst as sun-starts on a stream.
　　Yea, faileth now even dream
The dreamer, and the lute the lutanist;
Even the linked fantasies, in whose blossomy twist
I swung the earth a trinket at my wrist,
Are yielding; cords of all too weak account
For earth with heavy griefs so overplussed.
　　Ah! is Thy love indeed
A weed, albeit an amaranthine weed,
Suffering no flowers except its own to mount?

Ah! must —
Designer infinite! —
Ah! must Thou char the wood ere Thou canst
      limn with it?
My freshness spent its wavering shower i'
      the dust;
And now my heart is as a broken fount,
Wherein tear-drippings stagnate, spilt down ever
      From the dank thoughts that shiver
Upon the sighful branches of my mind.
      Such is; what is to be?
The pulp so bitter, how shall taste the rind?
I dimly guess what Time in mists confounds;
Yet ever and anon a trumpet sounds
From the hid battlements of Eternity;
Those shaken mists a space unsettle, then
Round the half-glimpsèd turrets slowly
      wash again.
      But not ere him who summoneth
      I first have seen, enwound
With glooming robes purpureal, cypress-crowned;
His name I know, and what his trumpet saith.
Whether man's heart or life it be which yields
      Thee harvest, must Thy harvest-fields
      Be dunged with rotten death?

Now of that long pursuit

Comes on at hand the bruit;

That Voice is round me like a bursting sea:

'And is thy earth so marred

Shattered in shard on shard?

Lo, all things fly thee, for thou fliest Me!

Strange piteous, futile thing!

Wherefore should any set thee love apart?

Seeing none but I makes much of naught'
　　(He said),

'And human love needs human meriting:

How hast thou merited—

Of all man's clotted clay the dingiest clot?

Alack, thou knowest not

How little worthy of any love thou art!

Whom wilt thou find to love ignoble thee,

Save Me, save only Me?

All which I took from thee I did but take,

    Not for thy harms,

But just that thou might'st seek it in My arms.

    All which thy child's mistake

Fancies as lost, I have stored for thee at home:

    Rise, clasp My hand, and come!'

  Halts by me that footfall:

  Is my gloom, after all,

Shade of His hand, outstretched caressingly?

  'Ah, fondest, blindest, weakest,

  I am He Whom thou seekest!

Thou dravest love from thee, who dravest Me.'

About the Artist

Though he lost an eye as a child, TIM LADWIG gravitated toward the visual arts and learned to draw. His parents encouraged him, supplying him with paper and pencils, and there always seemed to be room on the walls to hang his best work.

In college he studied academic painting and drawing in Italy and earned a bachelor of arts degree in graphic design from Wichita State University. He learned the mechanics of the graphic arts industry as an illustrator/designer in an advertising agency, where he worked for five years.

The Hound of Heaven is the fourth book Tim has illustrated. He is married to Leah, his honest critic and chief encourager. They have one daughter, Briana, and live in Wichita, Kansas.